50 BBQ Marinades for Flavor Packed Meals

By: Kelly Johnson

Table of Contents

- Classic BBQ Sauce
- Honey Mustard Marinade
- Teriyaki Marinade
- Spicy Chipotle Marinade
- Garlic and Herb Marinade
- Asian Sesame Marinade
- Lemon Pepper Marinade
- Balsamic Vinegar Marinade
- Sweet and Sour Marinade
- Maple Glaze Marinade
- Chimichurri Sauce
- Yogurt and Mint Marinade
- Mango Habanero Marinade
- Red Wine Marinade
- Curry Coconut Marinade
- Citrus Herb Marinade
- Peach BBQ Marinade
- Jamaican Jerk Marinade
- Spicy Peanut Marinade
- Cilantro Lime Marinade
- BBQ Whiskey Marinade
- Mustard and Brown Sugar Marinade
- Southwest Chipotle Marinade
- Ginger Soy Marinade
- Thai Peanut Marinade
- Rosemary Garlic Marinade
- Dill and Lemon Marinade
- Smoked Paprika Marinade
- Cilantro Jalapeño Marinade
- Maple Dijon Marinade
- Mediterranean Olive Oil Marinade
- Raspberry Chipotle Marinade
- Zesty Italian Marinade
- Curry Yogurt Marinade
- Honey Garlic Marinade
- Spicy Garlic Soy Marinade

- Red Pepper Flake Marinade
- Cumin Lime Marinade
- Black Pepper and Thyme Marinade
- Smoky BBQ Marinade
- Blueberry Balsamic Marinade
- Miso Marinade
- Orange Ginger Marinade
- Habanero Garlic Marinade
- Bourbon Brown Sugar Marinade
- Fajita Marinade
- Sesame Ginger Marinade
- Italian Dressing Marinade
- Sun-Dried Tomato Marinade
- Cilantro Avocado Marinade

Classic BBQ Sauce

Ingredients:

- 1 cup ketchup
- ¼ cup apple cider vinegar
- ¼ cup brown sugar
- 1 tablespoon Worcestershire sauce
- 1 teaspoon smoked paprika
- ½ teaspoon garlic powder
- ½ teaspoon onion powder
- Salt and pepper to taste

Instructions:

1. **Combine ingredients**: In a saucepan, mix all ingredients.
2. **Simmer**: Bring to a simmer over medium heat and cook for about 15 minutes, stirring occasionally.
3. **Cool and store**: Allow to cool before using or storing in the refrigerator.

Honey Mustard Marinade

Ingredients:

- ½ cup Dijon mustard
- ¼ cup honey
- ¼ cup apple cider vinegar
- 2 tablespoons olive oil
- Salt and pepper to taste

Instructions:

1. **Whisk ingredients**: In a bowl, whisk together all ingredients until smooth.
2. **Marinate**: Use as a marinade for chicken, pork, or vegetables for at least 30 minutes before cooking.

Teriyaki Marinade

Ingredients:

- ½ cup soy sauce
- ¼ cup brown sugar
- ¼ cup rice vinegar
- 2 tablespoons sesame oil
- 2 cloves garlic, minced
- 1 tablespoon grated ginger

Instructions:

1. **Mix marinade**: Combine all ingredients in a bowl and stir until sugar is dissolved.
2. **Marinate**: Use to marinate chicken, beef, or tofu for at least 1 hour before grilling or broiling.

Spicy Chipotle Marinade

Ingredients:

- ½ cup olive oil
- 2 tablespoons chipotle peppers in adobo sauce, minced
- 2 tablespoons lime juice
- 1 teaspoon cumin
- 1 teaspoon garlic powder
- Salt to taste

Instructions:

1. **Blend ingredients**: In a bowl, mix all ingredients until well combined.
2. **Marinate**: Use for chicken, shrimp, or vegetables and marinate for at least 30 minutes before cooking.

Garlic and Herb Marinade

Ingredients:

- ½ cup olive oil
- ¼ cup red wine vinegar
- 4 cloves garlic, minced
- 2 tablespoons fresh herbs (e.g., rosemary, thyme, oregano), chopped
- Salt and pepper to taste

Instructions:

1. **Combine ingredients**: In a bowl, whisk together all ingredients.
2. **Marinate**: Use for chicken, fish, or vegetables and marinate for at least 1 hour.

Asian Sesame Marinade

Ingredients:

- ½ cup soy sauce
- 2 tablespoons sesame oil
- 2 tablespoons rice vinegar
- 1 tablespoon honey
- 1 teaspoon grated ginger
- 2 cloves garlic, minced

Instructions:

1. **Mix marinade**: Combine all ingredients in a bowl and whisk until smooth.
2. **Marinate**: Use for chicken, beef, or vegetables for at least 30 minutes before cooking.

Lemon Pepper Marinade

Ingredients:

- ½ cup olive oil
- ¼ cup lemon juice
- 1 tablespoon lemon zest
- 1 teaspoon black pepper
- Salt to taste

Instructions:

1. **Whisk ingredients**: In a bowl, mix all ingredients until well combined.
2. **Marinate**: Use for chicken or fish and marinate for at least 30 minutes before grilling.

Balsamic Vinegar Marinade

Ingredients:

- ½ cup balsamic vinegar
- ¼ cup olive oil
- 2 tablespoons honey
- 2 cloves garlic, minced
- Salt and pepper to taste

Instructions:

1. **Combine ingredients**: In a bowl, whisk together all ingredients until well mixed.
2. **Marinate**: Use for chicken, pork, or vegetables and marinate for at least 1 hour before cooking.

Sweet and Sour Marinade

Ingredients:

- ½ cup soy sauce
- ¼ cup honey or brown sugar
- ¼ cup rice vinegar
- 2 tablespoons ketchup
- 1 teaspoon garlic powder
- 1 teaspoon ginger, minced

Instructions:

1. **Mix ingredients**: In a bowl, whisk together all ingredients until smooth.
2. **Marinate**: Use for chicken, pork, or tofu, and marinate for at least 1 hour.

Maple Glaze Marinade

Ingredients:

- ½ cup maple syrup
- ¼ cup soy sauce
- 2 tablespoons apple cider vinegar
- 1 teaspoon Dijon mustard
- 1 teaspoon garlic powder

Instructions:

1. **Combine ingredients**: In a bowl, mix all ingredients until well combined.
2. **Marinate**: Use for chicken or pork, and marinate for at least 30 minutes.

Chimichurri Sauce

Ingredients:

- 1 cup fresh parsley, chopped
- ¼ cup red wine vinegar
- ½ cup olive oil
- 4 cloves garlic, minced
- 1 teaspoon red pepper flakes
- Salt and pepper to taste

Instructions:

1. **Mix sauce**: In a bowl, combine all ingredients and stir until well mixed.
2. **Serve**: Use as a marinade for grilled meats or as a sauce.

Yogurt and Mint Marinade

Ingredients:

- 1 cup plain yogurt
- ¼ cup fresh mint, chopped
- 2 tablespoons lemon juice
- 2 cloves garlic, minced
- Salt and pepper to taste

Instructions:

1. **Combine ingredients**: In a bowl, mix all ingredients until smooth.
2. **Marinate**: Use for chicken or lamb, and marinate for at least 1 hour.

Mango Habanero Marinade

Ingredients:

- 1 ripe mango, pureed
- ¼ cup lime juice
- 1 tablespoon habanero sauce (or to taste)
- 2 tablespoons olive oil
- Salt to taste

Instructions:

1. **Blend marinade**: In a bowl, combine all ingredients and mix until well blended.
2. **Marinate**: Use for chicken or fish, and marinate for at least 30 minutes.

Red Wine Marinade

Ingredients:

- 1 cup red wine
- ¼ cup olive oil
- 2 tablespoons balsamic vinegar
- 4 cloves garlic, minced
- 1 teaspoon thyme

Instructions:

1. **Mix marinade**: In a bowl, whisk together all ingredients.
2. **Marinate**: Use for beef or lamb, and marinate for at least 1 hour.

Curry Coconut Marinade

Ingredients:

- ½ cup coconut milk
- 2 tablespoons curry powder
- 2 tablespoons lime juice
- 1 teaspoon ginger, minced
- Salt to taste

Instructions:

1. **Combine ingredients**: In a bowl, mix all ingredients until well combined.
2. **Marinate**: Use for chicken or shrimp, and marinate for at least 30 minutes.

Citrus Herb Marinade

Ingredients:

- ½ cup orange juice
- ¼ cup lemon juice
- ¼ cup olive oil
- 2 tablespoons fresh herbs (e.g., thyme, rosemary), chopped
- Salt and pepper to taste

Instructions:

1. **Mix ingredients**: In a bowl, whisk together all ingredients until combined.
2. **Marinate**: Use for chicken or fish, and marinate for at least 1 hour.

Peach BBQ Marinade

Ingredients:

- 1 cup peach preserves
- ¼ cup apple cider vinegar
- 2 tablespoons soy sauce
- 1 tablespoon Dijon mustard
- 1 teaspoon garlic powder

Instructions:

1. **Combine ingredients**: In a bowl, mix all ingredients until smooth.
2. **Marinate**: Use for chicken or ribs, and marinate for at least 1 hour.

Jamaican Jerk Marinade

Ingredients:

- 1 cup green onions, chopped
- ¼ cup soy sauce
- 2 tablespoons vegetable oil
- 2 tablespoons lime juice
- 1 tablespoon brown sugar
- 1 teaspoon allspice
- 1 teaspoon thyme
- 1-2 Scotch bonnet peppers (to taste)

Instructions:

1. **Blend marinade**: In a blender, combine all ingredients and blend until smooth.
2. **Marinate**: Use for chicken or pork, and marinate for at least 2 hours.

Spicy Peanut Marinade

Ingredients:

- ½ cup peanut butter
- ¼ cup soy sauce
- 2 tablespoons lime juice
- 1 tablespoon chili paste
- 2 cloves garlic, minced

Instructions:

1. **Mix marinade**: In a bowl, whisk together all ingredients until well combined.
2. **Marinate**: Use for chicken or tofu, and marinate for at least 1 hour.

Cilantro Lime Marinade

Ingredients:

- ½ cup fresh cilantro, chopped
- ¼ cup lime juice
- ¼ cup olive oil
- 2 cloves garlic, minced
- Salt and pepper to taste

Instructions:

1. **Combine ingredients**: In a bowl, mix all ingredients until well combined.
2. **Marinate**: Use for chicken or shrimp, and marinate for at least 30 minutes.

BBQ Whiskey Marinade

Ingredients:

- ½ cup whiskey
- ½ cup BBQ sauce
- ¼ cup brown sugar
- 2 tablespoons Worcestershire sauce
- 1 teaspoon smoked paprika

Instructions:

1. **Mix marinade**: In a bowl, combine all ingredients and stir until mixed.
2. **Marinate**: Use for beef or chicken, and marinate for at least 1 hour.

Mustard and Brown Sugar Marinade

Ingredients:

- ½ cup Dijon mustard
- ¼ cup brown sugar
- ¼ cup apple cider vinegar
- 1 tablespoon olive oil
- Salt and pepper to taste

Instructions:

1. **Combine ingredients**: In a bowl, whisk together all ingredients until well combined.
2. **Marinate**: Use for pork or chicken, and marinate for at least 1 hour.

Southwest Chipotle Marinade

Ingredients:

- ½ cup olive oil
- ¼ cup lime juice
- 2 tablespoons chipotle in adobo sauce
- 1 teaspoon cumin
- 1 teaspoon garlic powder

Instructions:

1. **Mix marinade**: In a bowl, whisk together all ingredients until smooth.
2. **Marinate**: Use for chicken or beef, and marinate for at least 1 hour.

Ginger Soy Marinade

Ingredients:

- ½ cup soy sauce
- 2 tablespoons fresh ginger, grated
- 2 tablespoons honey
- 2 tablespoons rice vinegar
- 2 cloves garlic, minced

Instructions:

1. **Combine ingredients**: In a bowl, mix all ingredients until well combined.
2. **Marinate**: Use for chicken or fish, and marinate for at least 30 minutes.

Thai Peanut Marinade

Ingredients:

- ½ cup peanut butter
- ¼ cup soy sauce
- 2 tablespoons lime juice
- 1 tablespoon honey
- 1 teaspoon garlic, minced
- 1 teaspoon ginger, grated

Instructions:

1. **Mix marinade**: In a bowl, whisk together all ingredients until smooth.
2. **Marinate**: Use for chicken, tofu, or shrimp, and marinate for at least 1 hour.

Rosemary Garlic Marinade

Ingredients:

- ¼ cup olive oil
- 2 tablespoons fresh rosemary, chopped
- 3 cloves garlic, minced
- 2 tablespoons balsamic vinegar
- Salt and pepper to taste

Instructions:

1. **Combine ingredients**: In a bowl, mix all ingredients until well combined.
2. **Marinate**: Use for chicken or lamb, and marinate for at least 1 hour.

Dill and Lemon Marinade

Ingredients:

- ½ cup olive oil
- ¼ cup lemon juice
- 2 tablespoons fresh dill, chopped
- 2 cloves garlic, minced
- Salt and pepper to taste

Instructions:

1. **Mix marinade**: In a bowl, whisk together all ingredients until blended.
2. **Marinate**: Use for fish or chicken, and marinate for at least 30 minutes.

Smoked Paprika Marinade

Ingredients:

- ¼ cup olive oil
- 2 tablespoons smoked paprika
- 2 tablespoons apple cider vinegar
- 1 tablespoon honey
- Salt and pepper to taste

Instructions:

1. **Combine ingredients**: In a bowl, mix all ingredients until smooth.
2. **Marinate**: Use for pork or chicken, and marinate for at least 1 hour.

Cilantro Jalapeño Marinade

Ingredients:

- ½ cup olive oil
- ¼ cup lime juice
- 1 cup fresh cilantro, chopped
- 1 jalapeño, seeded and minced
- 2 cloves garlic, minced

Instructions:

1. **Mix marinade**: In a blender, combine all ingredients and blend until smooth.
2. **Marinate**: Use for chicken or fish, and marinate for at least 1 hour.

Maple Dijon Marinade

Ingredients:

- ¼ cup olive oil
- ¼ cup maple syrup
- 2 tablespoons Dijon mustard
- 2 tablespoons apple cider vinegar
- Salt and pepper to taste

Instructions:

1. **Combine ingredients**: In a bowl, whisk together all ingredients until well combined.
2. **Marinate**: Use for chicken or pork, and marinate for at least 1 hour.

Mediterranean Olive Oil Marinade

Ingredients:

- ½ cup olive oil
- ¼ cup red wine vinegar
- 2 tablespoons oregano, dried
- 2 cloves garlic, minced
- Salt and pepper to taste

Instructions:

1. **Mix marinade**: In a bowl, whisk together all ingredients until blended.
2. **Marinate**: Use for chicken, fish, or vegetables, and marinate for at least 30 minutes.

Raspberry Chipotle Marinade

Ingredients:

- ½ cup raspberry jam
- ¼ cup apple cider vinegar
- 1 tablespoon chipotle in adobo sauce
- 2 tablespoons olive oil
- Salt and pepper to taste

Instructions:

1. **Combine ingredients**: In a bowl, mix all ingredients until smooth.
2. **Marinate**: Use for chicken or pork, and marinate for at least 1 hour.

Zesty Italian Marinade

Ingredients:

- ½ cup olive oil
- ¼ cup red wine vinegar
- 2 tablespoons Italian seasoning
- 2 cloves garlic, minced
- Salt and pepper to taste

Instructions:

1. **Combine ingredients**: In a bowl, whisk together all ingredients until well mixed.
2. **Marinate**: Use for chicken, pork, or vegetables, and marinate for at least 1 hour.

Curry Yogurt Marinade

Ingredients:

- 1 cup plain yogurt
- 2 tablespoons curry powder
- 1 tablespoon lemon juice
- 2 cloves garlic, minced
- Salt to taste

Instructions:

1. **Mix marinade**: In a bowl, combine all ingredients and mix until smooth.
2. **Marinate**: Use for chicken or tofu, and marinate for at least 1 hour.

Honey Garlic Marinade

Ingredients:

- ¼ cup honey
- ¼ cup soy sauce
- 2 tablespoons apple cider vinegar
- 4 cloves garlic, minced
- 1 teaspoon ground ginger

Instructions:

1. **Combine ingredients**: In a bowl, whisk together all ingredients until well blended.
2. **Marinate**: Use for chicken, pork, or shrimp, and marinate for at least 1 hour.

Spicy Garlic Soy Marinade

Ingredients:

- ½ cup soy sauce
- 2 tablespoons sesame oil
- 4 cloves garlic, minced
- 1 tablespoon chili paste
- 1 tablespoon brown sugar

Instructions:

1. **Mix marinade**: In a bowl, whisk together all ingredients until combined.
2. **Marinate**: Use for beef or chicken, and marinate for at least 30 minutes.

Red Pepper Flake Marinade

Ingredients:

- ½ cup olive oil
- 2 tablespoons red pepper flakes
- 2 tablespoons red wine vinegar
- 2 cloves garlic, minced
- Salt and pepper to taste

Instructions:

1. **Combine ingredients**: In a bowl, mix all ingredients until well blended.
2. **Marinate**: Use for chicken or vegetables, and marinate for at least 1 hour.

Cumin Lime Marinade

Ingredients:

- ¼ cup olive oil
- ¼ cup lime juice
- 2 teaspoons ground cumin
- 2 cloves garlic, minced
- Salt and pepper to taste

Instructions:

1. **Mix marinade**: In a bowl, whisk together all ingredients until smooth.
2. **Marinate**: Use for chicken or fish, and marinate for at least 1 hour.

Black Pepper and Thyme Marinade

Ingredients:

- ½ cup olive oil
- 2 tablespoons fresh thyme, chopped
- 1 tablespoon black pepper
- 2 tablespoons balsamic vinegar
- Salt to taste

Instructions:

1. **Combine ingredients**: In a bowl, whisk together all ingredients until well mixed.
2. **Marinate**: Use for chicken or beef, and marinate for at least 1 hour.

Smoky BBQ Marinade

Ingredients:

- ½ cup BBQ sauce
- ¼ cup apple cider vinegar
- 2 tablespoons smoked paprika
- 2 tablespoons brown sugar
- Salt and pepper to taste

Instructions:

1. **Mix marinade**: In a bowl, combine all ingredients and mix until smooth.
2. **Marinate**: Use for ribs or chicken, and marinate for at least 2 hours.

Blueberry Balsamic Marinade

Ingredients:

- ½ cup fresh blueberries
- ¼ cup balsamic vinegar
- ¼ cup olive oil
- 1 tablespoon honey
- Salt and pepper to taste

Instructions:

1. **Blend ingredients**: In a blender, combine blueberries, balsamic vinegar, olive oil, honey, salt, and pepper. Blend until smooth.
2. **Marinate**: Use for chicken or pork, and marinate for at least 1 hour.

Miso Marinade

Ingredients:

- ¼ cup miso paste
- 2 tablespoons rice vinegar
- 2 tablespoons soy sauce
- 1 tablespoon sesame oil
- 1 tablespoon ginger, minced

Instructions:

1. **Mix marinade**: In a bowl, whisk together all ingredients until smooth.
2. **Marinate**: Use for fish or chicken, and marinate for at least 30 minutes.

Orange Ginger Marinade

Ingredients:

- ½ cup orange juice
- 2 tablespoons soy sauce
- 1 tablespoon fresh ginger, minced
- 1 tablespoon sesame oil
- Salt to taste

Instructions:

1. **Combine ingredients**: In a bowl, mix all ingredients until well blended.
2. **Marinate**: Use for chicken or tofu, and marinate for at least 1 hour.

Habanero Garlic Marinade

Ingredients:

- ¼ cup olive oil
- 2 tablespoons lime juice
- 2 cloves garlic, minced
- 1-2 habanero peppers, finely chopped
- Salt and pepper to taste

Instructions:

1. **Mix marinade**: In a bowl, whisk together all ingredients until well combined.
2. **Marinate**: Use for chicken or shrimp, and marinate for at least 30 minutes.

Bourbon Brown Sugar Marinade

Ingredients:

- ¼ cup bourbon
- ¼ cup brown sugar
- ¼ cup soy sauce
- 2 tablespoons Dijon mustard
- 2 cloves garlic, minced

Instructions:

1. **Combine ingredients**: In a bowl, whisk together all ingredients until smooth.
2. **Marinate**: Use for pork or chicken, and marinate for at least 2 hours.

Fajita Marinade

Ingredients:

- ½ cup olive oil
- ¼ cup lime juice
- 2 tablespoons chili powder
- 1 tablespoon cumin
- 1 teaspoon garlic powder

Instructions:

1. **Mix marinade**: In a bowl, whisk together all ingredients until well blended.
2. **Marinate**: Use for steak or chicken, and marinate for at least 1 hour.

Sesame Ginger Marinade

Ingredients:

- ¼ cup soy sauce
- 2 tablespoons sesame oil
- 1 tablespoon fresh ginger, minced
- 2 cloves garlic, minced
- 1 tablespoon rice vinegar

Instructions:

1. **Combine ingredients**: In a bowl, whisk together all ingredients until well combined.
2. **Marinate**: Use for chicken or tofu, and marinate for at least 30 minutes.

Italian Dressing Marinade

Ingredients:

- ½ cup Italian dressing
- 2 tablespoons lemon juice
- 2 cloves garlic, minced
- 1 teaspoon dried oregano
- Salt and pepper to taste

Instructions:

1. **Mix marinade**: In a bowl, combine all ingredients and mix well.
2. **Marinate**: Use for chicken, pork, or vegetables, and marinate for at least 1 hour.

Sun-Dried Tomato Marinade

Ingredients:

- ½ cup sun-dried tomatoes, packed in oil
- ¼ cup olive oil
- 2 tablespoons red wine vinegar
- 2 cloves garlic, minced
- 1 teaspoon Italian seasoning
- Salt and pepper to taste

Instructions:

1. **Blend ingredients**: In a blender, combine sun-dried tomatoes, olive oil, red wine vinegar, garlic, Italian seasoning, salt, and pepper. Blend until smooth.
2. **Marinate**: Use for chicken or vegetables, and marinate for at least 1 hour.

Cilantro Avocado Marinade

Ingredients:

- 1 ripe avocado
- ¼ cup fresh cilantro, chopped
- 2 tablespoons lime juice
- 2 cloves garlic, minced
- Salt and pepper to taste

Instructions:

1. **Blend ingredients**: In a blender or food processor, combine avocado, cilantro, lime juice, garlic, salt, and pepper. Blend until smooth.
2. **Marinate**: Use for chicken, fish, or tofu, and marinate for at least 30 minutes.

www.ingramcontent.com/pod-product-compliance
Lightning Source LLC
LaVergne TN
LVHW081331060526
838201LV00055B/2567

9798330521616